RABBI DR. TZVI HERSH WEINREB
Executive Vice President, Emeritus

212.613.8264 *tel*
212.613.0635 *fax*
execthw@ou.org *email*

The wisest of all men, King Solomon, taught that "there is nothing new under the sun." This is certainly true of even many important Jewish books that are published nowadays. But every so often, we do encounter a work that teaches time-honored lessons in a dramatically new and authentically original manner.

The Three Images, by my respected colleague Rabbi Zev Shandalov, is one such book. Rabbi Shandalov fetches fresh water from the wellsprings of his own imagination. He uses the technique of imagery to evoke visual memories of his personal experiences and expands upon these images to impart lessons of great poignancy and powerful spirituality.

This book will interest, inform, and inspire the reader. The images themselves immediately gain the reader's interest. Rabbi Shandalov then builds a structure of educational bricks and mortar, based upon a dazzling variety of sources, so that the reader becomes better informed of the greatest Torah teachings. But most importantly, the reader comes away from each chapter inspired to improve his or her behavior and motivated to become a better person and a better Jew.

I recommend this excellent book to anyone interested in traditional truths conveyed with clarity, erudition, and even greater creativity.

Rabbi Dr Tzvi Hersh Weinreb
Executive Vice President, Emeritus
Orthodox Union
April 27, 2022

Preface

After serving for ten years as the Rabbi of Congregation Kehilath Jacob Beth Samuel (KJBS), our family made Aliya in July 2009. This Modern Orthodox shul located in Chicago, Illinois is the very same one where I grew up and prayed from the time I was a young boy all the way through adulthood. It is also the shul where I grew as an individual, a Jew and as a rabbi.

A shul rabbi's responsibilities include the preparation of thousands of speeches, *drashot* (sermons generally related to the weekly Torah portion) and classes. One area in particular that is an annual challenge to rabbis is the High Holy Day season. During this time, not only do they have to compose and deliver many speeches, but those speeches are expected to be the best and most inspirational of the year. After all, it is the time when most Jews are introspective and are indeed looking for the spark or inspiration that will motivate them.

As a result, many of my summers were spent crafting and authoring dozens of speeches. While I "felt" each and every word of every speech I wrote year round, I connected most to the ones I gave every year at *Kol Nidre*, the eve of *Yom Kippur*.

The reason I felt such an affinity to those speeches more than any other was due to a specific "formula" I had used successively for ten years. As you will read in the first chapter, I employed a method known as imagery. I spoke of three images I had seen during the course of the prior year that guided me to focus my energy and thoughts during Yom Kippur. Keeping those images in mind during *Tefilla* (the prayer services) always worked for me. Being mindful of those images, congregants shared that this method helped them focus their thoughts as well.

After ten years, with a total of thirty images and the stories that accompany them, I decided to write this book, which in a sense wrote itself.

I hope that you will enjoy the book and be inspired by the thoughts contained in its pages. I recommend that you read the chapters one at a time and allow yourself the chance to think about the imagery in each one. Clearly, some of the images will *seem* repetitious. However, each one is unique and contains a nuance that sets it apart from the others.

The beauty of this book is that you may read any chapter at random and be inspired by an image which can be incorporated into your personal life for further growth.

I wish to express my deepest gratitude to *HaKadosh Baruch Hu*, Who enabled me to write this book and Who enables me to accomplish anything at all in this world.

Without a doubt, my greatest inspiration in life is my *Eshet Chayil* (valorous wife), Andy. Without her, I would accomplish nothing. All I have and all that I give is merely as a result of having found my soulmate, my love and my life-source in her. From the day I considered entering the rabbinate until this very day, Andy has been supportive, encouraging, caring and, when necessary, a good critic. **She is truly my *Ezer K'Negedo* (helpmate), and it is to her that I dedicate my book.**

I also wish to thank my family, my parents Rabbi Ben ז"ל and Simmie Shandalov, תבלט"א, my daughters Daniella and her husband Benny Rabin, Ayelet and Eliana and her husband Shmuel for their lifetime of support and unconditional love. You mean the world to me!

My gratitude also goes to the officers, board members and general membership of Congregation Kehilath Jacob Beth Samuel.

I wish to thank my editor, Rachel Lobel, who took it upon herself to edit this book. Rachel spent incalculable amounts of time, painstakingly poring over each word and sentence. I am eternally grateful for her having transformed this volume that you now read.

Finally, I wish to thank the residents of Maale Adumim – my home in Israel – and in particular the neighborhood of Mitzpe Nevo. We have loved every minute and have been warmly welcomed into the community. I could not imagine living anywhere else.

Chapter
1

≈ Image One ≈

So much of what we do during the *Yamim Noraim* (High Holy Days), and specifically what we do on *Yom Kippur* (Day of Atonement), become meaningless if we are not in the proper frame of mind. Our mental attitude toward a particular life event can make or break how that event turns out. Take Olympic athletes, for example. They can train hundreds or thousands of hours prior to attempting certain tasks in the Olympic Games. However, if at the last moment, they are not ready mentally, then their performance will suffer. Our frame of mind completely dominates how we will succeed in an important event or face a particular challenge.

There is no day more important in our lives than *Yom Kippur*. This is the *Yom HaKadosh* (Holy Day) during which we stand before the Creator of the world and confess our sins and say that, despite all of our shortcomings, we want Him to overlook the past and let us continue with our lives. What day could impact our lives more?

It is this thought that has caused me great consternation over the years. While I do everything possible to prepare myself for this holy and awesome task – go to the *mikveh* (ritual bath), review the *Machzor* (festival prayer book), and even make a feeble attempt at *teshuva* (repentance) – there still seems to be something missing.

For years, I could not put my finger on it. One day it hit me. While I am *physically* preparing myself, I am not preparing myself *mentally* for this awesome day. How do I assure myself that my mind is involved in this process for the next twenty-five hours that comprise the holiest day of the year? After all, we have many things on our plates with which to be concerned. There are hundreds of other issues that can take over our minds during those twenty-five hours. So, it has always been a personal challenge to bring my mind to shul with me with the proper preparation, attitude and internal conviction.

Then, one day, something happened that finally gave me some insight into how to tackle this issue. I received a letter in the mail – certainly a common everyday occurrence.

How do you read your mail? If you are like most people, you turn the envelope over, slit it open and pull out what is inside. However, unlike most people, the first thing I do is look at the return address. Why is that? Because the *source* of the letter is what is of primary importance to me. If I see that the return address contains any indication of a mass mailing or a hint of something unimportant, the envelope doesn't even warrant being opened and gets tossed into the recycling bin.

One day in 1985, I was getting ready to read my mail in the usual fashion by first looking at the return addresses. And then it happened. Staring me right in the face in black and white were the words: **INTERNAL REVENUE SERVICE.** My heart skipped a beat. My pulse quickened. I turned pale, and my breath came in short spurts. All of this just because of a return address. The thought that they might just be sending me a letter to see how I was feeling never crossed my mind. All I could imagine was Leavenworth Prison and a court ruling of 5-10 years hard labor – all this before I even opened the envelope. Yet, I know that I had always been honest in filling out my tax returns. What power the return address and the name had on me and my psyche!

As it turned out, the IRS was simply requesting something quite insignificant. This experience led me to ask why it had had such a strong, visceral reaction on me. What had instilled such *fear* in me? It was the realization – founded or unfounded – that the IRS could have the power to alter my life. If, in fact, I had made a grave error and "cheated" on my taxes, there could have been serious repercussions affecting my entire life.

I then took the next logical step in my thought process. If I had reacted to the possibility of my life being altered by the IRS merely by the return address on the envelope, how could I not react with the same fear and trepidation regarding *Yom Kippur*?

The truth is that this fear should grip me a hundredfold on *Yom Kippur*.

In reflection on this most awesome day, *I know* that I have not acted properly during the previous year. *I know* that *Hashem* (G-d) can alter my life. I *know* that when I see the calendar change from *Elul* to *Tishrei* (two Hebrew months ushering in the High Holy Day period), it is time for me to step up and explain myself and ask for forgiveness.

So, it was many years ago when I made a conscious decision to think of this envelope on the night of *Kol Nidre*. It helped me to put things in perspective.

After realizing the power of that imagery, I sought out other images during the year and decided to reflect upon them, as well, prior to and on *Yom Kippur*.

≈ Image Two ≈

The second image is a distinct memory. It was September 28, 1971, and Chicago was being pummeled by a heavy thunderstorm. Normally, that would not be cause for alarm, but that day was *Erev Yom Kippur* (the Eve of the Day of Atonement). Thousands of people stood by their windows and doors to see if the rain and winds would let up so they could get to the shul for the holiest night of the year. And then, just a minute or two after candle lighting, it became calm – no rain, no wind – only an eerie silence permeated the air. With confidence and gratitude to *Hashem*, we all walked to *shul* (the very one where I would one day serve as rabbi). No sooner had we arrived, than the electricity went out. Imagine standing in preparation for *Kol Nidre* and suddenly there is no light at all in the *shul*.

As it was getting late, and the time to begin the services was drawing closer and closer, someone ran to the kitchen and lit some candles to place by our *Chazzan* (cantor), Rabbi David Silver (of blessed memory), so that at least *he* would be able to read the words of the *Machzor*. The problem was that although *he* could read the words, no one else in *shul* could see his own *Machzor* to read the *tefillot*.

What were we going to do?

The decision was made that Rabbi Silver would read every single word out loud, and the congregation would repeat after him – including the *Shemoneh Esrei* (the central prayer said silently while standing).

I must tell you that, even as I sit here writing these words, a chill goes down my spine when I think of that night. It was, without a doubt, the most spiritual and special *Kol Nidre* of my life and of many of those present. What made the service different than any other? I believe it served as a paradigm for what the day is all about. We were *all* in the dark. We did not know what we were going to do. There was much confusion and murmuring. Then, as if guided by heavenly ministers, our entire *kehilla* (congregation) banded together – every single person – and *davened* as a united group. We all approached G-d unified as one people.

This was the message of *Yom Kippur* to me that night and still serves as an annual reminder to me. We are in the dark before *Yom Kippur*. We are confused by our past. We are trembling from the knowledge that we are lost in a world of the darkness of sin. What are we going to do? Then, a light goes on – a single light that allows us to become unified, that symbolizes the light of redemption from our sins and reassures us of life in the coming "new year." This wasn't felt individually. It was felt and experienced by a unified congregation.

It is this memory that I carry with me *each and every Kol Nidre night since my youth*. Memories of powerful experiences from a past *Yom Kippur* can serve as a springboard every year to put us in the proper frame of mind.

≈ IMAGE THREE ≈

Finally, there is one more image that I have found helpful over the years, which is one we see in front of us on this holy day. It is recalling the words of a certain *tefilla*.

Perhaps, one of the most well-known *tefillot* in the *Rosh Hashana/Yom Kippur* liturgy is *B'Rosh Hashana Yikateivun* ("On Rosh Hashana they will be inscribed"). We clearly state in this prayer what decisions are being made by *Hashem* on this day.

Listen, as if it were for the first time, to the words of this moving prayer:

בְּרֹאשׁ הַשָּׁנָה יִכָּתֵבוּן. וּבְיוֹם צוֹם כִּפּוּר יֵחָתֵמוּן. כַּמָּה יַעַבְרוּן. וְכַמָּה יִבָּרֵאוּן. מִי יִחְיֶה. וּמִי יָמוּת. מִי בְקִצּוֹ. וּמִי לֹא בְקִצּוֹ. מִי בַמַּיִם. וּמִי בָאֵשׁ. מִי בַחֶרֶב. וּמִי בַחַיָּה. מִי בָרָעָב. וּמִי בַצָּמָא. מִי בָרַעַשׁ. וּמִי בַמַּגֵּפָה. מִי בַחֲנִיקָה וּמִי בַסְּקִילָה. מִי יָנוּחַ. וּמִי יָנוּעַ. מִי יִשָּׁקֵט וּמִי יְטֹרֵף. מִי יִשָּׁלֵו. וּמִי יִתְיַסָּר. מִי יֵעָנִי. וּמִי יֵעָשֵׁר. מִי יֻשְׁפָּל. וּמִי יָרוּם:

On Rosh Hashana they will be inscribed, and on Yom Kippur they will be sealed; how many will pass from the Earth and how many will be created; who will live and who will die; who will die at his predestined time and who before his time; who by water and who by fire, who by sword, who by beast, who by famine, who by thirst, who by storm, who by plague, who by strangulation, and who by stoning? Who will rest and who will wander, who will live in harmony and who will be harried, who will enjoy tranquility and who will suffer, who will be impoverished and who will be enriched, who will be degraded and who will be exalted?

I have often wondered why this list includes something that appears to be redundant. We say כַּמָּה יַעַבְרוּן וְכַמָּה יִבָּרֵאוּן (how many will pass from the Earth and how many will be created), and then we say

מִי יִחְיֶה וּמִי יָמוּת (who will live and who will die).

Aren't we really saying the same thing twice? Aren't we in effect asking who is going to survive the coming year and who will not? Why the need to say both of these phrases? And then it occurred to me. They are making two very different statements. When we say מִי יִחְיֶה וּמִי יָמוּת, we are referring to the actual life or death which *Hashem* decides this day. But when we say כַּמָּה יַעַבְרוּן וְכַמָּה יִבָּרֵאוּן, we are saying something completely different. כַּמָּה יַעַבְרוּן asks who will just pass through this life. Who is it that will pass through and leave no mark, will have no impact, and will not accomplish anything? Who will have written on his tombstone: *Died at age 30, buried at age 70*?

The other side of this coin is וְכַמָּה יִבָּרֵאוּן. Who will in fact make use of his life to create a legacy and make a difference in his life and the lives of countless others? So, we are bidden on *Yom Kippur* to not just **pass** through life but to **live** life to its fullest potential and be **creative** with our lives.

This is the other thought that goes through my mind on *Yom Kippur*. The image of those words on the pages of the *Machzor* leads me to ponder: Do I want only to pass through this life or do I want to make a difference in this world? It is the power of the day of *Yom Kippur* that bids us to think about making that decision and provides us with the choice to act upon it.

Chapter 2

≈ Image One ≈

While the following story is well known, it is powerful and instructive as the first image of this chapter.

A water bearer in India carried two large pots – one hanging on each end of a pole.

One pot was perfect and always contained a full portion of water at the end of the long walk from the stream to the mistress's house, while the other pot was cracked and arrived only half full.

This went on daily for a full two years, with the bearer delivering only one and a half pots full of water to her mistress's house.

The perfect pot was proud of its accomplishments, perfect to the end for which it was made. But the poor cracked pot was ashamed of its own imperfection and miserable that it was able to accomplish only half of what it had been made to do.

After two years of what it perceived to be a bitter failure, the cracked pot spoke to the water bearer one day by the stream: "I am ashamed of myself, and I want to apologize to you."

"Why?" asked the bearer. "What are you ashamed of?"

"For these past two years, I have been able to deliver only half my load; because this crack in my side causes water to leak out all the way back to your mistress's house. Because of my flaws, you have to do all of this work and don't get full value from your efforts," the pot said.

The water bearer felt sorry for the old cracked pot, and in her compassion she said, "As we return to the mistress's house, I want you to notice the beautiful flowers along the path."

Indeed, as they went up the hill, the old cracked pot took notice of the sun warming the beautiful wild flowers on the side of the path, and this cheered it to some extent.

However, at the end of the trail, it still felt bad. It had leaked out half its load, and so again, it apologized to the bearer for its failure.

The bearer said to the pot, "Did you notice that there were flowers only on your side of the path, but not on the other pot's side? That's because I have always known about your flaw, and I took advantage of it. I planted flower seeds on your side of the path; and every day while we walk back from the stream, you've watered them.

For two years, I have been able to pick these beautiful flowers to decorate my mistress's table. Without you being just the way you are, she would not have this beauty to grace her house."

This story or, more specifically, the cracked pot in this story is indeed an image to which all of us can relate. We can look at our flaws and our shortcomings and feel bad and choose to let them ruin our self-image. We can look at these flaws and decide that they define who we are.

Contrarily, we can take a step back and see how we can correct our flaws and shortcomings. For those we just cannot seem to correct, we can begin to concentrate on how to use what *seem* to be flaws or shortcomings and use them to our advantage. On *Yom Kippur*, we must see this image of the cracked pot and think of our flaws and contemplate: **How do I work with my issues and with my flaws? How do I find a way to** serve *Hashem* even with my shortcomings? At the same time, I must consider how I can use my strengths to serve *Hashem* even better.

When we consider this idea and ponder how we can turn our flaws and imperfections into tools to be used to serve *Hashem*, we accomplish two tasks. On the one hand, we begin to make personal changes. On the other hand, we put our *emunah* (faith) into practice. We accept that *Hashem* gave each of us certain abilities. By using them in the way they were meant to be used, we will improve our relationship with *Hashem*. Both of these actions are of utmost importance for our growth in terms of *bein adam l'Makom* (between man and G-d) and in terms of *bein adam l'atzmo* (between man and himself). In addition to these aspects, we work as well on our *bein adam l'chavero* (between man and fellow man). We take these flaws, turn them into advantages and use them to help our fellow man.

≈ Image Two ≈

The second image is based on an oft-cited Gemara (*Brachot 28:*) that records a conversation between Rabban Yochanan Ben Zackai and his students.

וכשחלה רבן יוחנן בן זכאי, נכנסו תלמידיו לבקרו...אמרו לו: רבינו, ברכנון אמר להם: יהי רצון שתהא מורא שמים עליכם כמורא בשר ודם. אמרו לו תלמידיו: עד כאן? ־ אמר להם: הלוואי תדעו, כשאדם עובר עבירה אומר: שלא יראני אדם.

And when Rabban Yochanan ben Zackai fell ill, his students entered to visit him. ...They said to him: Master, bless us. He said to them: May it be [Hashem's] will that the fear of heaven shall be upon you like the fear of flesh and blood. His disciples said to him: Is that all? He said to them: If only [you can attain this]! You can see [how important this is], for when a man wants to commit a transgression, he says, I hope no man will see me.

While we walk around with an awareness that **people** can see what we are doing, sadly, we are not always aware of **Hashem's** constant presence. Lest you think that this is a recent phenomenon, note well that Rabban Yochanan ben Zackai dealt with this centuries ago.

What did Rabban Yochanan ben Zackai mean when he exclaimed: "If only!"? He understood human psychology and how we all think. On one level, we already know that a certain act may be wrong, which is why we offer a silent prayer that we hope no other human being will see us as we do "the deed." The automatic erroneous implication, therefore, is that *Hashem* will not see us, so we are safe to do what we want. Not only are we fooling ourselves, but we are also relegating *Hashem* to the backseat. It is as if we are saying that He cannot see us.

This lack of awareness leads us all to sin and leads us down a path that *Hashem* has told us not to travel. This is a large part of what *Yom Kippur* is about. We are asking our Father in Heaven to forgive us for **forgetting** Him. We are asking Him to pardon us for not being aware of Him in our day-to-day lives. He asks us to love Him, and we ignore Him. He asks us to spend time with Him, and we act as if He is not there.

The image of the words of Rabban Yochanan ben Zackai should haunt us. It should propel us to want to raise our awareness of *Hashem* in our lives. By doing so, as he says, we will forge a stronger bond with *Hashem* and reduce our chance of sinning. It will also increase our *Ahavat Hashem* (love of G-d) to serve Him with joy.

≈ Image Three ≈

The final image is my *Zaydeh's* (grandfather's) watch. Although I grew up in Chicago, much of my family – including my maternal grandparents – lived in Toronto. We saw each other two or three times a year at most, but the relationship between them and our Chicago family was a close one. In the days before internet, email and cell phones, our method of communication was letters and occasionally a phone call. While we all built a strong relationship with them, I was especially close to my *Zaydeh*, Shmuel Aharon Posner, z"l.

In May of 1973, the inevitable happened: my *Bubbie* (grandmother) passed away. Then in February of 1974, my *Zaydeh* passed away. I was devastated by the death of my *Bubbie*, as she was the first person close to me who had died; but with the death of my *Zaydeh*, I was crushed. It was the end of an era on my mother's side of the family. Although I was only 15 years old, there was a gaping hole in my heart that I felt would never heal.

My family flew to Toronto for my *Zaydeh's* funeral. From the airport, we went straight to his apartment. I began to look around the rooms. I could hear his voice, feel his love and see his mark everywhere. Then I walked into his bedroom. On his bed was his clothing, and I realized that those were the last things he had worn on this Earth. Next to his clothing was his watch. I picked it up and held it in my hand. It was at that moment that I felt the gravity of his loss so acutely, and I began to wail inconsolably.

I held his watch in my hand for what seemed like an eternity, and I cried like never before. I did not want to let go of it. As a matter of fact, for some inexplicable reason, it was as if I *couldn't* let go. Perhaps in my youthful mind, letting go of his watch was like letting go of *Zaydeh*.

Over the past many years, I have thought back to that day and that moment. What was it about that watch, and how had I become so close to my grandfather who lived nearly 850 kilometers away?

As I got older, I understood that the watch represented the time my *Zaydeh* was here on this Earth. And, at the moment when he died, his time stood still. In a certain sense, so did mine, with all my memories of him frozen in time. But what about the long distance between us and the infrequent visits? How was it that, in spite of the distance and separation, we had been so close?

Then it dawned on me: love doesn't know any distance. No matter how far apart we were, it was love that bound us together. While there was a *physical* distance between us, there was absolutely no *spiritual* distance between us.

I took this idea to the next step, and that is the reason why his watch is the third image. The same is true for our relationship with *Hashem*. In the times that we had a *Bet HaMikdash* (Holy Temple), we visited *Hashem* three times a year through the *mitzvah* (commandment) of *Aliya l'Regel* (pilgrimage). Nowadays, some "see" Him frequently, while others see Him infrequently. However, for all of us, *Hashem* is not *physically* present; and in that sense, He is **very** distant. In a spiritual sense, He is very close to us. *Love knows no distance. Hashem* is always with us and as close as we choose.

It is essential to realize that *Hashem is as close to us as we let Him be.* That is what I learned from my *Zaydeh's* watch and what I think about on *Yom Kippur.*

Let us remember that we are always under *Hashem's* watchful gaze. Let us remember to think about our shortcomings and how to change them to positives. We must always keep in mind that *Hashem* loves our efforts, always sees our positive deeds and embraces us with fatherly love. Finally, let us remember that *love knows no distance.*

Chapter
3

≈ Image One ≈

The first image is a tower. In 2006, I went to Poland with a group of rabbis. It was a grueling and emotionally-filled experience. At various points, I was overcome with sadness, grief and horror. I don't know if I could do it again, but I am glad that I had taken that trip.

Being in Poland, I had the opportunity to visit many concentration camps. Just after entering the gates of Birkenau (Auschwitz II), we climbed the stairs to a tower. It looked no different than many other towers we had seen that day, with its windows and sparse furnishings. However, this one turned out to be quite different. Here we stood in the same spot where the Nazi guards must have stood as they watched the *Kedoshim* (holy martyrs) enter via transport trains into the camp.

What I saw from the tower made me shudder. At a distance of 300 meters was a platform where endless trainloads of doomed passengers had been forced to disembark from their last trip anywhere. The tower guards had had a clear view of these Jewish souls as they formed a line in front of the commandant. Standing with them as silent sentries were two sets of train tracks – the left one bringing trains loaded with their holy human cargo and the right one allowing the empty trains to exit the camp in order to bring back more Jewish souls. What must the tower guards have observed in 1942? Likely they would have observed men, women and children receiving instructions in which line to stand: one to slave labor and the other to the gas chambers. In other words, as I stood in that tower, I could see – in the most literal sense – life-and-death decisions being made right before my eyes.

The next time you are in shul during *Yom Kippur*, observe that life-and-death decisions are being made there as well.

Why do the Jewish people go to *shul* on *Yom Kippur* – on the *Yom HaKadosh*, the holiest day of the year? It is the day on which *Hashem* makes decisions of life and death – yours and mine.

Unlike the monsters who stood guard and made decisions in the death and slave camps, *our* Guard is a *Dayan Emet* (a True Judge). He sits on His heavenly throne with love, compassion and mercy.

It is this idea that crossed my mind as I stood in that guard tower. It was as if I were witnessing a *Yom HaDin* (Judgment Day). I closed my eyes and tried to imagine that terrifying moment. I wondered what must have gone through the minds of the terrified men, women and children – all the Jewish souls standing in the scorching heat or the freezing cold. I came to the conclusion that on their minds at that fateful moment was **life** or **death** – of their parents, spouses, children and, of course, their own.

This idea is reminiscent of *U'Netaneh Tokef* ("Let us speak of the awesomeness") – one of the most inspiring passages that we read on *Rosh Hashana* and on *Yom Kippur*. In that paragraph, we make reference to the fact that all human beings pass before G-d on this day *"kivnei maron"* (like sheep) who pass before their shepherd for his inspection. So, too, we pass before G-d on this day for Him to inspect us.

That was the feeling I had as I gazed out of the guard tower window to the platform below. It is this feeling that we must experience as we stand before G-d on the holiest day of the year.

Do we sit in shul thinking of when we can break the fast, where our next vacation will be or if we have the latest app on our phone? Do we truly grasp the importance and gravity of why we are praying and what fate we are facing? It took my standing on a platform in a Nazi guard tower to come to this realization.

Try to imagine the feelings of fear, trepidation and anxiety – the fear of the unknown – as those holy Jews stood on the platform passing in front of the Nazis. Now, *l'havdil elef alfei havdalot* (in total contradistinction), try to imagine yourself standing before G-d as it is your turn to pass before Him, *kivnei maron*. How does it feel? Close your eyes and feel that moment. That is, indeed, what we must feel on *Yom Kippur*.

≈ IMAGE TWO ≈

The next image is that of a mourner. It was June 18, Erev Shabbat, during the summer of 2008. News circulated that Simcha Davis, a young member of the Chicago Jewish community, had been in a serious car accident. Not knowing whether Simcha would live or die, the call went out all over the world to say *Tehilim* for him.

Shabbat came, and no one other than those in the hospital knew whether Simcha was still alive. That Shabbat happened to be *Rosh Chodesh* (the head of the month) *Tammuz*. Sadly, Simcha passed away that fateful Friday night and was buried on Sunday.

At the funeral, one of Simcha's brothers said the following: *"We didn't know what was happening. We didn't know if Simcha was alive or not. That Shabbat morning we davened. And although it was Rosh Chodesh,* **we davened like it was Yom Kippur.** *Each and every word jumped out at us and took on new meaning."*

"It was Rosh Chodesh, but we davened like it was Yom Kippur."

And what about when it actually is *Yom Kippur*?

Do we daven like it is *Yom Kippur*? Are we just going through the motions and reading the words out of the *Machzor* without understanding them?

Do we wander in late to *shul* at 10:00 or 11:00 in the morning as if it were just another day?

Do we concentrate on the prayer as if our lives were hanging in the balance?

When we go to *shul* on *Yom Kippur, it is Yom Kippur* and we need to pray like it is *Yom Kippur*. We get chances to daven 365 days a year, but we only have one *Yom HaKadosh* per year and *Yom Kippur* is it. "It was *Rosh Chodesh* but we davened like it was *Yom Kippur*." The image of this mourner and this phrase will ring in my ears forever.

We still have this chance to stand before *Hashem*, to deal with what we have not done and what we have yet to do. We have this chance to realize that it is not too late to change our future, because it is indeed in our hands to do so.

≈ Image Three ≈

Finally, I want to share a story about a machine gun. On a group trip to Israel one summer, we had the privilege to meet Mrs. Cheryl Mandel, an amazing woman who told us about her son, Daniel, a commander in the IDF. On one particular day, his platoon had surrounded a building where some suspected terrorists were hiding. They had announced that all persons in the house must come out, as the IDF was about to enter. Suddenly, shots rang out and Daniel was gunned down and died instantly.

Cheryl also told us a wonderful story about her son that left a big impression on me. Before he was a commander, Daniel was in basic training in the IDF. Part of the training included long treks with heavy packs, weapons and other equipment. One of the soldiers was responsible for carrying a machine gun that weighed approximately 90 pounds. He trained with successively heavier guns to build up the strength necessary to carry the weighty machine gun.

There were still another 65 kilometers to go until the end of this particularly long trek, and the soldier carrying the machine gun tripped and fell. Daniel immediately ran to help him up, despite the fact that part of the training was to figure out how to right oneself without assistance. The commander punished Daniel for interfering by ordering him to take over carrying the

90-pound gun (which weighed almost as much as he did) for the rest of the trek.

Daniel had not been prepared at all for such a grueling task, but he managed to carry the gun the entire distance without complaining.

Daniel's mother concludes with a poignant thought. The day her son was gunned down in cold blood, she thought of this story. She and her family were not trained nor were they prepared to carry such a heavy load in life. They had no time to adjust to the idea that their son had been killed in cold blood. Despite the long and burdensome journey facing them, they were going to continue on life's road without complaining. It is what was thrust upon them and they would have to adapt.

What an inspiring story. When I heard it, it reminded me of so many conversations I have had with people after their own tragedies. In one way or another, all of us have things thrust upon us for which we are unprepared. At times, we are all put in a situation similar to Daniel – one that could literally or figuratively break our backs.

If we persevere and carry that load with us to the finish line, and if we do not succumb to the temptation to give up, then we will have learned what *Hashem* is seeking to teach us. Everything happens for a reason. We may not understand it. We are permitted to question *why* things happen. We are permitted to seek reasons and answers. However, when we see life through the prism of *Emuna* (faith), as Cheryl Mandel did, we will all be stronger and more able to get through life with acceptance and peace.

Chapter 4

≈ Image One ≈

The first image is that of a cell phone. Shortly after *Sukkot* (Festival of Tabernacles) one year, I was held up at gunpoint. Actually, I was held up at *two* gunpoints, and it made me reflect on the thought that I had had my own very *personal* and traumatic *Yom Kippur*.

It was about 9:30 pm, and I had just finished meeting with a group of people. I was walking to my car; and as I put my key in the door to unlock it, a shadow came over me. I turned around expecting to see one of the people from the meeting, but was stunned to see a man standing there with a gun pointed at me.

As he approached me, he noticed the cell phone in my hand. At that same moment, I was so shocked that I dropped the phone without realizing it. I gave him my wallet (a normal thing to do when a gun is held to your head), and he then demanded my cell phone. "Give me the phone! I said give me the cell phone!" I was certain that my life was going to end, and all over a cell phone. He became more agitated, and then a second man approached with his gun aimed at my head as well. I was thinking about my family and how I would never see them again. In that eternity of a millisecond, I wondered what it would feel like to die. What would it be like to be one of you and hear about my death – and all over a cell phone?

Then in the next instant, I realized that my Palm Pilot™ was in my jacket pocket. I flipped him my jacket, and again, he demanded the cell phone. I yelled back that I had just given it to him, hoping that he would touch the pocket and think it was the phone. He did. It was obvious – and providential – that brains had not been generously doled out to him. The second man actually cursed me and told me to run. I expected that he was going to shoot me in the back, but, Baruch Hashem, he did not.

The rest of the story is secondary. I do not know how many of you have come face to face with what seemed like certain death?

I *did*…and I *do* know how it feels…

It made me realize that life truly can end in an instant. I have always known this intellectually. Now, however, I knew it viscerally, as well. One never knows when the time that *Hashem* has given us on this Earth will come to an end.

My appreciation for life, my family and *Hashem* changed dramatically that night.

We all come face to face with our own mortality on *Yom Kippur*. It is true that there is no gun being held to our heads. Instead, there are a couple of books that sit open before *Hashem* – the Book of Life and the Book of Death. We all need to pay close attention to those books and what they mean for each of us.

≈ *Image Two* ≈

Next is the story of an airplane, which occurred shortly after I was held up at gunpoint. I had been to Russia with a group of rabbis. We were settling in to our seats on the flight from Moscow back to Israel. Despite being exhausted after our four-day jaunt in the Former Soviet Union, we felt exhilarated that our next stop would be Israel.

The pilot received clearance from the tower, and we began to head down the runway. The view out of our windows was like something from an old spy-novel. The ground and the plane were covered in ice. It was snowing heavily, with most of it blowing sideways due to fierce winds. The pilot brought the plane to top speed, as he approached the end of the runway. Suddenly, he hit his brakes so hard that everything that wasn't attached went flying and people began to scream. Even the flight attendants began to cry. As the pilot continued putting pressure on the brakes, I actually said the phrases from the conclusion of the *Yom Kippur* service known as "*Shemot*" (it includes the *Shema* and acceptance of *Hashem* as our King).

I immediately flashed back to a few short months ago when I had been held up at gunpoint. I remembered the many people who asked if I had recited the *Shema*. Then I had not, but this time I did remember.

I was certain that we were going to crash into another plane because of the snow, ice and wind.

I mentally said goodbye to my family for the second time in these few short months.

I believed, again, that I was staring death in the face.

I wondered, again, what it would feel like to die.

I saw, again, that life could end in an instant.

And with all the gratitude to *Hashem* that I could muster, I once again survived the incident. My appreciation for surviving both of these incidents has markedly changed my outlook on life.

Our mortality is not something that we wish to face every day, if at all; and just the mere fact of thinking about it indicates that our lives will, indeed, end one day. That is a scary thought to contemplate. However, if we do not contemplate it at least on *Yom Kippur*, then we are not acknowledging one of the most important aspects of the day. On occasion, we do need to consider that our life on this Earth is time bound. For some people, that thought occurs when they are confronted by a family member who is terminally ill. For others, it is when they themselves fall ill. For all of us, this idea needs to be on the top of the list on *Yom Kippur*, because it helps us to realize the gravity of the day and the importance of our prayers.

≈ Image Three ≈

The final story is that of a baby. Every single day, hundreds of thousands of babies are born into this world. Unfortunately, there are many people for whom the idea of having a baby brings feelings of desperation each month, as they are unable to conceive. This amazing story about one couple in Memphis, Tennessee will inspire you.

The couple was married for several years and had not been able to have children. They sought medical help and spiritual help, and they received support from friends. All of this went a long way to help their psyche but not to conceive a child. They resigned themselves to the fact that they were not meant to become parents.

And then, one day, their lives took an amazing turn. They received the news they had been longing to hear for years: "You are pregnant!"

Like many couples who had been waiting to have a child, they were elated.

Like many couples who had been waiting to have a child, they were anxious.

Like many couples who had been waiting to have a child, they were telling everyone the good news to share in their joy.

However, unlike most other couples waiting to have a child, they endured not three years, nor five years, nor even ten years, but 31 years.

Just as life can come to an abrupt end in a single instant, the hopes and dreams of a couple can become reality in a single instant. Against seemingly impossible odds, they brought a new life into this world.

As we are told in Midrash Lekach Tov on Megillat Esther, Yeshuat Hashem k'heref ayin (*Hashem's* salvation can come in the blink of an eye).

All of us, at one time or another, are faced with situations that seem hopeless. We feel that there is no chance in the world that we will get that job, or that our proposal will be accepted, or that our child will find the appropriate help.

At this point, you may be asking yourself why even bother to change? I am who I have been my whole life, and it will take a miracle to make any change. However, if you keep working at discovering your true self, then with the help of *Hashem* you can transform yourself. It may take you more time than for others, but with His help, anything is possible. Remember that *Yeshuat Hashem k'heref ayin*. In the blink of an eye, *Hashem's* power is manifested in our lives – we get that job, the proposal is accepted, and the child gets the needed help.

While we may sit in *shul* with a sense of hopelessness and a feeling of helplessness, we must realize that G-d is an active Creator working in our daily lives. The concept of *Hashgacha P'ratit* (Divine providence/personal oversight by G-d) is not relegated just to Him helping us find our partner in life. His watchful eye helps us even when *we* think a situation is hopeless.

Where there is Hashem, there is always hope.

I don't often use personal vignettes to illustrate a point or to awaken a certain feeling. On *Yom Kippur*, the rules are different. On *Yom Kippur*, we all must pause and think about our own lives. On *Yom Kippur*, we must realize that for those 25 hours or so we are, indeed, "on trial."

These images will be with me, personally, more than just for *Yom Kippur*. I do not wish *my* experiences on anyone. However, if you can even for a moment feel what it must have been like, you can begin to get a sense of what we should be experiencing over the *Yom HaKadosh*. Not a sense of *fear* per se, but a feeling of *this is it, a feeling of awe*. My life is actually on the line and *Hashem* is making decisions today.

On the other hand, I *do* wish for you the same elation and joy that this couple in Memphis must have felt at the birth of their child. Those feelings are also appropriate for *Yom Kippur*. We all have done many things wrong over the course of the past year. Yet, we all have the right to feel a sense of elation when *Hashem* looks down at all of us and says סלחתי כדבריך (I have forgiven you as you have requested).

Chapter
5

≈ Image One ≈

The first image is *Tefillat HaDerech* (Traveler's Prayer). The day was June 25, 2006, corresponding to 29 Sivan. Like the start of any other day, soldiers around Israel prepared to begin their day. Unfortunately, it would not be just any ordinary day. It would become a "bookmark" in time. It would be the day that the Middle East began to boil over once again.

On that morning, Gilad Shalit was taken captive by Hamas. Israel entered Gaza with the intent of locating and retrieving her lost comrade. Hour by hour, the process became more deadly.

A short time later, word came that two more Israeli soldiers (Eldad Regev and Ehud Goldwasser) had been taken captive in the North. The situation on both fronts reached a boiling point. Katyushas rained down on our northern border towns, and we were forced to enter Lebanon in order to eradicate Hezbollah and to return our soldiers. Unfortunately, we did not accomplish either task, and many of our soldiers were killed.

While a lot of ink could be spilled writing about this war, that is not my purpose at this point. The focus instead will be placed on a short video clip sent to many during this war. It brought tears to the eyes of all who watched it.

The camera pans in on the interior of a crowded tank, with four or five soldiers inside. By the light of a flashlight, one of the soldiers begins to recite the *Tefillat HaDerech* aloud. This prayer is normally recited before any journey, particularly when leaving one location for another and even if there does not seem to be any danger.

However, the soldier in this video clip is not reading *Tefillat HaDerech* like someone taking off in an airplane. He is not reading it like a driver leaving Jerusalem. He is reading it with a full heart, knowing that it may be the last prayer he says in this world.

Everyone in his tank crew is listening and going through the same emotions.

I chose this image to share because of the feelings that these individuals must have had at that moment. They were davening knowing that their lives were at stake. They were davening with probably the most *kavana* (intention) they had ever had.

We must keep in mind that you and I are all on a journey... one that we call "life," as we pass through this world and on to the next world. Our daily prayers act as a daily *Tefillat HaDerech* as well.

People sit in the sanctuary of their respective *shuls* davening, in many cases, no differently than they did six months ago; no differently than they davened *Shacharit* (the morning prayer) or *Maariv* (the evening prayer) on any other day of the year. Why is that? Many people approach *Yom Kippur* with very little thought.

Today, we are about to embark on a new journey for the new year. Our prayers on *Yom Kippur* are the *Tefillat HaDerech* for the upcoming year.

Deep down, you should be asking yourself the same question you asked six months ago: *Why is this night different from all other nights?*

The answer on *Yom Kippur* is much less complicated than it was six months ago. On the night of *Kol Nidre*, the answer is that G-d Himself has given us an opportunity to right the wrongs of the past. During those 25 hours of *Yom Kippur*, G-d Himself says "I am available to you now more than ever." But to *know* it and to *feel* it are two different things.

If we begin to *feel* it inside – if we begin to internalize the importance of the day and how our lives hang in the balance – then our *davening* will not be the same during *Yom Kippur* as the rest of the year.

We must see ourselves in the same situation as the tank commander saying the *Tefillat HaDerech*. We must think of ourselves in the same mortal danger and facing the same vicissitudes of life as those fine Israeli soldiers. That sense of importance can and will make all the difference in our *davening* and how it is received in *Shamayim* (Heaven).

≈ IMAGE TWO ≈

The next image is a visitor's pass. For months, on my *shtender* (lectern) in my *shul* in Chicago, I kept a hospital visitor's pass to room 225 in Children's Memorial Hospital. This pass was from the day I visited a 12-year-old boy named Yehiel Mael. I knew Yehiel and his family from the neighborhood and wished to visit him. He was hospitalized due to a serious head injury. I entered his room with trepidation not knowing what I would see.

What I found was nothing short of a miracle. Here was a boy who, only a few days earlier, had been hit in the head by a moving car as he peeked into traffic to see if it was safe to cross the street. When Yehiel's mother told him that I had entered the room, he said, "I know, I recognized his voice." I thought I would cry right then and there.

Here was a boy who, for all normal medical reasons, could easily have been taken from this world; and he **knew** that I had entered the room. He was moving around in an agitated state, which was another good sign that he was alive. Yehiel was only a few months away from his Bar Mitzvah, and **all** of that could have changed in an instant.

His progress was already a miracle, and he would go on to amaze his doctors and community with a remarkable recovery.

In August of that same year, I happened to be at the Kotel and saw Yehiel there putting on *Tefillin* for the very first time. The boy, who was in a state of "touch and go" at the beginning of June, was at the Kotel to put on *Tefillin* at the beginning of August.

I held on to that visitor's pass, and I looked at it before every single *tefilla*. I reminded myself that *we are all given a visitor's pass when we are born.*

Throughout life, we get battered and bruised. Like Yehiel, we too can recover with *Hashem*'s help. Like Yehiel, the goal is to end up at the Kotel forging a closer relationship with God.

We come, we visit this world, and then we leave.

רבי יעקב אומר העולם הזה דומה לפרוזדור בפני העולם הבא. התקן עצמך בפרוזדור, כדי שתכנס לטרקלין

(Rabbi Yaakov said: this world is like a hallway leading to the Next World. Prepare yourself in the hallway in order to enter into the Great Hall)

The belief that our lives are fleeting and that our time in this world can be up at any moment is **not** an easy concept to grasp; it is not one that we **wish** to grasp.

It is this visitor's pass that I look at every day to remind myself how fleeting life can be and how we need to cherish each and every moment.

≈ Image Three ≈

The final image is a mix-up. The following article appeared in many newspapers in early June 2006:
Whitney Cerak and Laura VanRyn looked remarkably alike, both attractive young women with blond hair, similar facial features and the same build and height.

They were together the night of April 26, returning from banquet preparations with a group from Taylor University, when a tractor-trailer slammed into their university van, peeling off the side and killing five people. Cerak's family was told their 18-year-old was among the dead. VanRyn's parents were told their 22-year-old daughter was alive but seriously injured and in a coma. The VanRyns kept vigil at the young woman's bedside for weeks; but as she gained consciousness, she began saying things that didn't make sense. This week, they made a stunning discovery: the recovering patient wasn't their daughter at all. She was Whitney Cerak."I still can't get over it. It's like a fairy tale," said Cerak's grandfather Emil Frank. VanRyn's parents, who had kept a daily Web log of the young woman's recovery after the crash, disclosed the mix-up on their blog."Our hearts are aching as we have learned that the young woman we have been taking care of over the past five weeks has not been our dear Laura," the family wrote."Certainly there are those people that are devastated today because the person, their friend, who *they thought had lots of hope and was progressing every day, they now found out she has died."*

"There are also those who are rejoicing because Whitney is alive."

I cannot begin to imagine what both families must have felt as the news of the true identities was discovered. Finding out that your loved one is alive instead of dead. Finding out that your loved one is dead rather than alive. How very painful it must have been. And the world shakes its collective head in disbelief and wonders how this could have happened.

The truth is that this happens every day of our lives. Not to the same degree or publicity as this case, but, it does happen countless times a day.

Stop and think for a moment. For those few days, *only Hashem* knew the true identities of those two young women. Everyone else thought they knew who they were dealing with. Everyone thought they knew what was happening and what they were facing.

The truth is that this happens to us all the time. We are dealing with an individual in business, we are dealing with a friend, we are dealing with a family member, and then they turn out to be someone completely different. We thought we could trust them, we thought they were a true friend, we thought they loved us and *we thought we knew who they were.* And during this entire time, as we thought we were dealing with *one* person, it turned out to be a *different* person. All along, only *Hashem* knew the true identity of this individual.

As devastating as these experiences must be, we must realize that we truly don't always know who "the other person is." We must also recognize that, relative to the rest of the world, each of *you* is the *other* person. Ask yourselves if people really know the *true* "you"? Nine times out of ten, the answer is "no." And why is that? Because often we are afraid to show who we really are for fear of rejection, ridicule or any other myriad reasons.

While everyone sitting next to you does not know your real and true identity, *Hashem* does. Even if you do not know *your own self*, He does. And it is at this moment in time that each of us must stop and face that persona and deal with the "*real me.*" On *Yom Kippur*, there can be no hiding behind a mask. We call the Day of Atonement *Yom HaKippurim* – or as some say, a day *like Purim* – because we have a mask on. It is time to remove the mask and deal with who you are as you approach *Hashem*.

Chapter 6

≈ IMAGE ONE ≈

Let's begin with "the piece of paper." Thanks to the Jewish Federation of Metropolitan Chicago, I had the opportunity to be in Hungary one winter. I was witness to some amazing history and culture of the Hungarian Jews of today and of the past few hundred years. While I was there, I saw one item that I was certain would serve as one of the Three Images.

The piece of paper I refer to was called a *"Schutz-Pass."*

Rauol Wallenberg (may his memory be for a blessing) is widely celebrated for his successful efforts in having rescued tens of thousands of Hungarian Jews from the Nazis and the Fascists during the later stages of World War II. While serving as Sweden's special envoy in Budapest between July to December 1944, Wallenberg issued protective passports and sheltered Jews in buildings designated as Swedish territory.

To accomplish this, Wallenberg invented a special Swedish passport known as the *Schutz-Pass*. It was a colorful, imposing, official-looking document. With permission from no one, he announced that it granted the holder immunity from deportation to the death camps. Wallenberg distributed his *Schutz-Pass* indiscriminately to Jews. The *Schutz-Pass* alone is credited with saving more than 20,000 Jewish lives.

Using his American funds, Wallenberg scoured Budapest for buildings to rent. He eventually found thirty-two, which he declared to be "extra-territorial buildings" protected by Swedish diplomatic immunity. He found a way "to place 35,000 people in buildings designed for fewer than 5,000."

Think about it for a moment. Without the *Schutz-Pass*, it meant almost certain death. With the *Schutz-Pass*, it often meant being safe from the Nazis.

A simple piece of paper. And on *Yom Kippur*, we speak not only of a piece of paper but of entire books: the Book of Life and the Book of Death.

What will help determine in which book we will be inscribed? A lot will depend on what we have written on our own *Schutz-Pass* during the past year. Remember that that piece of paper made the difference between life and death. If it had the wrong information, it was useless and would then, quite likely, mean death.

On *Yom Kippur*, we must review the "piece of paper" we have been writing on for the past year to see whether we have acted correctly and performed enough good deeds to enable us to be written in the Book of Life?

The *Schutz-Pass* gave Jews the possibility of a second chance at life, even though the pass itself did not represent who they truly were. So too, on *Yom Kippur*, *Hashem* gives us this "pass" to enable us to merit longer and richer lives.

≈ IMAGE TWO ≈

A taxi. The following story takes place on the second day of *Rosh Hashana* 5768/2008. My family finished our *Seudat Chag* (holiday meal) at my in-laws' house, and we were walking home. Along the way, I saw a friend of mine and his wife sitting on their front porch; so we stopped to chat for a few minutes

Suddenly, out of nowhere, a man ran past me and up the porch where my friend and his wife were sitting. My friend asked this harried individual, "Nu? What was it?" And the man cried out, *"It's a boy!"* I quickly learned that he was related to our friends.

The next exchange between them blew me away:

"When was he born?"

"NOW"....

"What do you mean now?"

"NOW....right here...right now...in the **TAXI** right here!"

This lovely couple was on the way to the hospital to deliver their baby and to drop off their other two children to be watched by my friends. The baby did not want to wait and was delivered, literally, as they pulled up to my friends' house. Emergency services were called, and it is the ensuing few minutes that I will never forget.

This man, whom I had never met before, was Rabbi Moshe Steinberg. We shared this incredible moment together, and I gave him a big hug and *Mazal Tov* (congratulations). My wife ran to get water for the new parents. We just could not wipe the smiles off of our faces.

Within minutes, a small crowd gathered. Shouts of *Mazal Tov* rang out, as the paramedics put the mother and new baby into the ambulance. We waved as the ambulance pulled away, and everyone felt elated.

The following Friday night was the child's *Shalom Zachor* (celebration on the first Friday night after a male child is born). I was asked to speak that evening, and this is what I said:

The *Daf Yomi* (daily page of Talmud) for the very day this child was born was *Ketubot* 12a-b. On that *daf* it says:

היתה מעוברת, ואמרו לה מה טיבו של עובר זה?

The *Gemara* (Talmud) is discussing a certain baby that was still in his mother's womb in determining what his *halachic* (legal) status is.

For the purposes of this image, the details of what I said are not relevant. My point was to ask about the status of the child whose birth we had just experienced. The truth is that his status was already self-evident. He had brought instant *Ahavat Yisrael* (love for a fellow Jew) into this world.

Thirty-six hours earlier, I did not even know the Steinbergs. Now, I sat at a *Shalom Zachor* and was thrilled to be sharing in the *simcha* (happy occasion) of our new-found friend. The next day, I joined in the *Brit Milah* (ritual circumcision) for little Mordechai Eliezer. What a thrill.

I share this image with you, because love for a fellow Jew that comes instantly not only fosters *Ahavat Yisrael* but *Ahavat Hashem* (love of G-d), as we are all His children. That is what we need to think about on *Yom Kippur*.

In the time of the *Mishkan* (the Tabernacle), every Jew over 20 years old had to bring a *Machatzit HaShekel* (a half-shekel coin) in order to be counted in the census. It is axiomatic to say that each person brought a half shekel because, by himself, an individual is merely that – an individual. By bringing a half shekel, it indicated he was a part of something bigger, something better. This idea fostered the idea of *V'ahavta l're'echa kamocha* (love your fellow Jew as yourself). This would also have an effect on *tefilla*, *achdut* (unity) in the community and in so many other areas of life.

Consider that while there are negative things that happen in the blink of an eye, there are also many beautiful things that occur suddenly as true gifts from *Hashem*. As a loving parent, *Hashem* wants to give us such gifts. Sometimes these gifts are overt, like this new-found friendship, and sometimes they are covert. In any case, *Hashem* is always sending us these "messages." We just need to open our eyes.

The year 5768 was a leap year, known in Hebrew as a *shana m'uberet* ("pregnant" year). Each of us needs to ask מה טיבו של עובר זה (what is the status of this coming "pregnant" year)? We have made, and will continue to make, promises to *Hashem* about the coming year. However, each of us needs to stop for a moment each day of this "pregnant year" and ask מה טיבו של עובר זה - am I living up to what I said I was going to do?

≈ Image Three ≈

The final image is a pair of *Tefillin*. There were times when I would wake up so early on Sunday or would have to leave town, that I was forced to *daven Shacharit* elsewhere and not in the *shul* where I was the rabbi. It so happened that, on one hot Sunday, I woke up very early and did not want to wait until 7:30 am to *daven* in my *shul*. So I ended up going to another *shul*.

When we reached *Yishtabach* (a prayer in the morning service), a man walked in who – by all appearances – had not spent any time learning in *Kollel* (advanced study group). I found it hard to believe he was even Jewish, and here he was carrying a *Tefillin* bag and a pointy *kippah* in his hand. As I continued to *daven*, I kept one eye on my *siddur* and the other on this man.

As I looked at him, I began to sense that he was going through a major change in his life. I was not sure what made me think this. I don't mean a major change such as becoming a *baal teshuva*. I mean a major change that was turning his life upside down. I am not minimizing any actions of *baale teshuva*. I am merely suggesting that this situation I was witnessing was unique. After a few minutes of watching him struggle to put on his *Tefillin*, it finally dawned on me why I had such a feeling. As he slipped his *shel yad* (the straps that are wound around one's arm) over his arm and began to tighten the knot, he made two additional motions that most people do not make when putting on *Tefillin*. He first squeezed his left hand into a very tight fist. Then he took the *Tefillin* strap and, before winding it around his arm, he held the strap between his teeth to help tighten the knot.

This man was using a similar set of actions that an addict uses when injecting drugs into his system – tightening the fist and holding the strap for making a tourniquet to inject drugs. This man, who in all likelihood was a recovering drug addict, was sitting in a shul and putting on *Tefillin*. Not only that. He was making the exact same physical movements used to take drugs (the fist and the teeth) and was turning it around 180 degrees to put on *Tefillin*. This is an image I will never forget.

What a lesson it taught me and can teach you as well. We do things we should not do. We all do things that make us feel embarrassed, at the very least, and ashamed at the worst. Yet, we have the capacity and ability, like this man, to change all of that. We can take one action and replace it with the opposite as a cure for the sin we might be doing.

We often hear the expression "to turn your life around." What exactly does that entail? For some, it might mean a more solid commitment to religion, to one's spouse, or to changing a host of other character traits.

It can be taken almost literally as well. We can take an action that was used for an improper reason and turn it around (like the man in the story) to use it for the proper reason.

Examples are numerous. Instead of speaking *lashon hara* (gossip), use that same capacity to *daven* better. Instead of using your mind to cheat another person, use that intellect to help someone improve his business. On *Yom Kippur*, it is time to face your demons.

On *Yom Kippur*, it is time to face up to your transgressions and not only think about them but decide to take action as well.

Chapter 7

≈ Image One ≈

Let's begin with a bumper sticker. As we drive down any street, we are constantly assaulted by hundreds of visual images. One of the icons of travel is the ubiquitous bumper sticker.

Many companies have vehicles that sport a fairly common bumper sticker: "How's my driving? Call 800-555-1212." I had never paid much attention to this particular sticker and never called one of the companies to comment.

Once, on a trip in Israel, I happened to read a bumper sticker that took on a whole new meaning for me. It read in Hebrew, "איך אני נוהג?" The simplest and most obvious translation is: "How am I driving?" On a much deeper level, it can translate to: "How am I acting?" (as in the well-known Talmudic phrase עולם כמנהגו נוהג, meaning that the world maintains its constant action).

This bumper sticker got me thinking. איך אני נוהג? – how am *I* acting? Am I acting in accordance with what *Hashem* wants me to do in this world? Am I treating my fellow man the way I am supposed to, or am I doing things to make *Hashem* or my fellow man upset? איך אני נוהג? Each and every one of us must ask ourselves this question on a daily basis.

This is the pertinent issue on the day of *Yom Kippur*. The truth is that, if you take stock of yourself by asking this self-examination question every day, you will have much less reason to ask for forgiveness. By this action alone, you can make corrections to your behavior and prevent your life from spinning out of control.

If part of the *Yom Kippur* experience is self-examination, then we must not only ask this question of ourselves on the *Yom HaKadosh* but on every single day of our lives. ‎איך אני נוהג?

I would even go a step further. The purpose of a bumper sticker is to be seen by the people behind you. Imagine if you are wearing such a sticker on the back of your shirt and the people behind you can call a number and actually tell you how they think you are acting. Instead, in our mind's eye, let's picture that the only one who can see this sign is *Hashem* Himself. How would *He* answer when we ask *Him* this question: ‎איך אני נוהג?

Just as the way you drive affects other people, so, too, your actions as you "drive" through life affect others. All of us need to be considerate of others as we drive down the asphalt road. Even more so do we need to be considerate of others as we travel down the road of life.

≈ IMAGE TWO ≈

The second image is one that you may have experienced many times in your life, but it is a situation from which we can all learn. I have a friend, who I will call David, and he is a real estate broker. He told me the following story about himself:

David had made a deal regarding his real estate sales commission with a particular manager. His years of loyal service to the organization had earned him a larger commission per each sale.

This particular manager was promoted to a different branch of the company, and David had a new boss. When it came time for the company to pay him for his most recent transactions, there was a dispute between David and his new manager regarding the amount of the commission. David pointed out to the new manager that a deal existed *on paper* indicating that he would get a certain commission. However, the circumstances as to how that was to be implemented were ambiguous. A confrontation ensued. David, who had worked for this company for over twenty-five years, was having his integrity questioned. They decided together to call his old boss, who verified that everything the new boss was being told was in fact true. In other words, David was due the greater amount of money.

After they hung up the phone, the new boss was still not comfortable with the situation and once again seemed to question David's integrity. Not wanting to escalate what had already become an all-out war, David decided to take a walk around the block. He was considering all of his options: "Do I go back inside and work for a man who seemingly does not trust me? Do I quit? How can I quit with a wife and children to support?"

David was mulling over all of this, when he literally bumped into a former co-worker. This colleague had opened his own business and had remembered David as a warm and intelligent individual. They sat and began to reminisce about the good times they had shared.

Suddenly, David's friend blurted out, "You're perfect!" Taken slightly aback by this outburst and considering that no one had ever told him he was perfect, David was somewhat baffled. "What am I perfect for?" He was told that given his experience, his knowledge of the real estate market and his ability to communicate well, David was perfectly suited to be the team trainer that he was looking for. Not only that, but this man said **he never would have thought of David had he not bumped into him at that moment.**

Let's reconstruct this scenario. Go back in time to the moment right before David bumped into his former colleague. He is down; he is faced with a crisis and is unsure of what to do. BAM! Into that potentially harmful thought process walks this opportunity of a lifetime. By the way, David did take the job.

Why do I share this image with you? Often, we walk around this planet thinking that *we* are in control and that *we* are making the world go 'round. Then, sometimes covertly and sometimes overtly (like for David), G-d reminds us that, at what seems our darkest hour, He is right there standing at our side and helping us through our lives and *He* is the one running the show. No, it does not always happen as clearly as it did in David's case. However, *Hashem* is always there. We just need to open our eyes.

≈ Image Three ≈

The final image is a mirror.

One morning, I took out the mirror that I keep with my *Tefillin* to see if they were straight on my head. As I did so, I noticed a smudge on my face and grabbed a tissue to wipe it off. To my dismay, when I looked back in the mirror, the smudge that I had seen a second ago was still there. I tried to wipe it off again from my face. On third glance, still seeing the smudge, it finally dawned on me that it was not on my face but actually on the mirror.

The smudge on that mirror reflects how society views each one of us. Do you buy into that idea, or are you comfortable as you are? If you look at that mirror and accept what you see as factual, then you will always see yourself as "smudged."

I smiled to myself and began davening. Only afterwards did it hit me what symbolism there was in that moment in front of the mirror. As an earlier image, I mentioned the concept of self-introspection with the question of איך אני נודה. However, we have to be careful to make an honest self-assessment based on real and positive feedback we get from ourselves and others. If another person's view of us is "smudged," or our own view is flawed based on a faulty self-assessment – and we reflect that internally and outwardly to others and allow ourselves to believe that this is who we are – then we are doing more damage than good.

When the *meraglim* (spies) went into Canaan to spy on the land, they made the following comment:

וְשָׁם רָאִינוּ אֶת־הַנְּפִילִים בְּנֵי עֲנָק מִן־הַנְּפִלִים וַנְּהִי בְעֵינֵינוּ כַּחֲגָבִים וְכֵן הָיִינוּ בְּעֵינֵיהֶם

("And there we saw the *Nephilim*, the sons of *Anak*, who come from the *Nephilim*; and we were in our own eyes as grasshoppers, and so we were in their eyes") *Bamidbar* 13:33

When we read this *pasuk*, we note that they said "we were in our own eyes as grasshoppers" – insignificant grasshopper-like individuals. By extension, that is how the spies were perceived by the inhabitants of Canaan. Why? Because if we have a smudged view of ourselves, that is what is being projected to others.

While this may be a nice lesson in psychology, what does it have to do with the night of *Yom Kippur*? Quite simply, this may be the key to the difference between being able to do *teshuva* or not. If we buy into the negative self-image we often have, we begin to question our ability to do *teshuva* in the first place. If I am as bad as people think I am (because of the smudged image I am transmitting to them), then how will *Hashem* love me enough to accept my *teshuva*? How will I be able to stand in front of him, let alone be worthy of His forgiveness, if I am as bad as I see myself in that mirror?

So, pull out that bottle of glass cleaner and start to clean your mirror. Understand that **NOTHING** stands in the way of *teshuva*. Listen to the words of the *Sefer Orchot Tzadikim*:

אבל אם עשו תשובה - אין לך דבר שעומד בפני התשובה. ולא יחשוב אדם: הואיל וחטאתי והחטאתי אחרים, לא אוכל לשוב. ומרפה ידו מן התשובה - חלילה מעשות זאת. כי אמרו בפרק חלק (סנהדרין קב א): אפילו ירבעם שחטא והחטיא - הקדוש ברוך הוא אמר לו: עתה תשוב. ולא רצה.

("But if they did *teshuva*, there is nothing standing in the way of your *teshuva*. I should not think that, since I have sinned and have caused others to sin, I cannot properly repent. I may then slacken off and not repent – Heaven forbid from thinking like this. For it says in the chapter of "*Chelek*" in the Tractate of *Sanhedrin* (102a) that even Yeravam ben Nevat, who sinned and caused much sinning, was told by G-d to repent immediately – but he chose not to.")

Who was Yeravam ben Nevat? He was a king of Israel a few generations after King David. He worshiped idols and influenced most of *Bnei Yisrael* to do so as well. Almost every time his name is mentioned in *Sefer Melachim* (Book of Kings), he is referred to as a *choteh u'machti* ("a sinner and one who causes others to sin"). And yet... He is still permitted to do *teshuva*.

Yes, look into that mirror, but never let your self-image compromise who you truly are. Always remember that, unlike the famous line about never being able to go home again, you are always welcome home to the house of *Hashem* and His loving embrace.

Chapter
8

≈ *Image One* ≈

The early part of the 21st century was not a particularly easy one in the Land of Israel. The attacks on buses, in the streets, cafes and other establishments wreaked havoc on daily life. A string of tragedies was left in the wake of this violence. For those who were living outside of Israel, it was painful and difficult. For those living in Israel, it was unbearable.

As time progressed, there seemed to be a certain routine that was followed in the aftermath of these murderous attacks. Often it included immediate rebuilding and placing memorial plaques commemorating those who had been murdered. After a period of time, booklets started to appear which included pictures of victims with their names and brief biographies. All of those *Kedoshim* (holy souls), of course, have their own stories. One that hit me particularly hard was the picture of little Shalhevet Pass (*hy"d*).

On March 26, 2001, at 4:00 pm, Shalhevet was shot in her stroller while her parents were walking from the parking lot in the Avraham Avinu neighborhood of Hevron where they lived. A Palestinian terrorist fired from the Abu Sneineh neighborhood on the opposite hill; and Shalhevet was killed instantly, as the bullet penetrated her head and passed through her skull. With blood running down her hands, the baby's mother grabbed her and ran. Shalhevet's young father, Yitzchak Pass, a student, who had been pushing the stroller, was also seriously wounded just minutes later by two bullets.

Less than a year later, I stood in the very spot where Shalhevet was murdered. I imagined her sitting in the stroller before the attack. I imagined her parents taking a nice afternoon walk with her and perhaps even planning her future. What would she have been like had she lived? What would have been her chosen career path? Whom would she have married and how many kids would she have had? Neither her parents nor anyone will ever know the answers to these questions.

It is this image of Shalhevet that I see as I recite the words in the *tefilla* of *Avinu Malkenu*:

אָבִינוּ מַלְכֵּנוּ, חֲמוֹל עָלֵינוּ וְעַל עוֹלָלֵינוּ וְטַפֵּנוּ.

אָבִינוּ מַלְכֵּנוּ, נְקֹם לְעֵינֵינוּ נִקְמַת דַּם עֲבָדֶיךָ הַשָּׁפוּךְ.

(Our Father, our King, have mercy upon us and upon our children and infants. Our Father, our King, avenge the blood of your servants that has been spilled.)

When we turn to G-d in terms of both *Avinu* (our Father) and *Malkenu* (our King), sometimes it is difficult to think on these lofty plains. What helps is putting a face to the idea and the request. In that vein, we turn to G-d and almost scream out: *Our Father, our King, please, we beg You to have pity and mercy! If not on us, if we are not deserving, then on the little children! Why do they need to suffer? Why do families need to become bereft of their little children?*

Dear G-d, we need Your mercy, we need Your compassion. Please, dear Father, heed our pleas!

≈ Image Two ≈

The next image is another very personal one, but sadly, one to which many can connect.

The date was 2 Av 5762 (July 11, 2002), and it was going along like any other lazy summer day. That is, until I received "the phone call." The caller told me to brace myself for some tragic news, and I instantly felt myself go weak. I had no idea what to expect, but no one ever wants to hear those words.

The tragic news was revealed. The eldest son of my closest friend had been killed in an automobile accident. Yaakov Matanky, who had not yet reached his 20th birthday, was on a country road in Wisconsin driving for the camp where he was working. He was killed instantly in a head-on collision with a truck. When I heard the news, I felt as though the world had stopped. My head began to spin. My thoughts turned to his parents, lifelong friends, and the horrific event that had just occurred and that would resonate for years.

With great trepidation, I picked up the phone to call the Matankys. I couldn't make the call. I hung up and tried to breathe. What do I say to them? Then, I tried again – one ring, two rings. Yaakov's father answered. All I could do was cry; all he could do was cry. The pain was palpable, and we just cried some more.

Then the next day, I had to watch two of my closest friends bury their eldest son. Without a doubt, after the death of my grandparents, this was the saddest day of my life. I had known Yaakov even before he was born.

Yaakov was eulogized by his father, as he stood at the pulpit in the shul where he serves as rabbi. This was the very same pulpit where he stood wishing his son *Mazal Tov* on his *Bar Mitzva*. It was the pulpit that he had hoped one day to wish his son *Mazal Tov* on the occasion of his *aufruf* (the Shabbat before an Ashkenazi wedding when the groom is called to the Torah) – a day that would never come.

It is this image that haunts me. Indeed, it was tragic for the family and for the entire community, but it is what it represented that continues to haunt me.

In such palpable terms, it represented the *frailty of life*. We all say that life is too short. Many young adults feel that they are invincible and that they will live forever. They think that nothing can happen to them. In the blink of an eye, all of that can come to an end.

We ask *Hashem* for life, for *chaim*. But what do we think of when we ask for this? What indeed is "life"? Do we realize that the day of *Yom Kippur* is the day when that decision of life or death is being made? It became painfully clear to me at Yaakov's funeral that life-or-death decisions are made for people of all ages, whether they are nineteen or ninety-five. We pray for *life* and not death.

Don't take life for granted. A young man with many years left ahead of him to contribute to this world was gone. For the rest of us, we really do not know what tomorrow will bring.

≈ Image Three ≈

The final image is a poem or, perhaps more correctly, a poetic piece of prose.

After the disaster of September 11, 2001, much ink was spilled in describing the thoughts and feelings of thousands of individuals. One evening, shortly after the horrific events of that day, I went online to search for something and came across the following piece attributed to Tess Haranda :

Have you ever thought, "Where was God on 9/11 when the World Trade Center and the Pentagon were attacked?" Well, I know where my God was on the morning of September 11, 2001, and He was very busy!

He was discouraging people from taking those four flights. Together they could accommodate more than 1,000 passengers, yet there were only 266 aboard. He was on those four flights giving the terrified passengers the ability to stay calm. Not one of the people who was called by a loved one on one of the hijacked planes mentioned that passengers were panicked, nor was there any screaming in the background. And on one of the flights, God gave strength to the passengers to overcome the hijackers.

God was also busy creating obstacles to prevent people who worked in the WTC from getting to work on time. The work day had begun, more than 50,000 people worked in the two towers, yet only 20,000 were at their desks. On that beautiful morning, God created scores of unexpected traffic delays, subway delays, and commuter train delays. A PATH train packed with commuters was stopped at a signal just short of the WTC and was able to return to Jersey City. And far more meetings were scheduled elsewhere than was usual.

God held up each of the two mighty towers for a half hour so that the people on the lower floors could get out. And when He finally let go, He caused the towers to fall inward rather than to topple over, which would have killed so many more people. The foundations of six surrounding buildings were demolished by the fall of the towers, but God held them up for many hours until all the occupants were safely evacuated.

And when the WTC and Pentagon buildings went down, my God picked up almost 3,500 of His children and carried them to their home for all eternity. He also sat down and cried that 19 of His children could have so much hate in their hearts that they did not choose Him, but another god that doesn't exist, and now they are lost forever.

He sent people trained in dealing with earthly disasters to save those who were injured. And he sent in thousands of others to help in any way they were needed. And He brought people together across the world in a way that moved thousands to tears and hundreds of thousands to prayer – and caused millions to turn to the one true living God.

He still isn't finished. Every day He comforts those who lost loved ones. He is encouraging others to reach out to those who don't know Him or believe in Him. He is giving the leaders of our great nation the strength and conviction to do the right thing, to follow His will, not a popular poll.

So if anyone ever asks, "Where was your God on 9/11?" you can say, "He was everywhere! And, in fact, he is everywhere *today and every day."* Without a doubt, this was the worst catastrophe most of us have ever seen. I can't imagine getting through such a difficult time without God at my side. Without God, life would be hopeless.

I must have re-read this piece at least ten times. It is powerful and says it all.

G-d *was* there on September 11. And that itself is the image. *Hashem* is with you as you sit in the sanctuary of a *shul*. He is with you in your car, your house and in your school. *Hashem* is everywhere, or as the Kotzker Rebbe once famously remarked: "*Hashem* is anywhere you let Him in." Isn't this something we all learned as little children? What is the novel idea here?

In the *Musaf Shemona Esrei* on *Rosh Hashana*, there is a *pasuk* from *Sefer Yeshayahu* (44:6) that reads

כֹּה־אָמַר יְהֹוָה מֶלֶךְ־יִשְׂרָאֵל וְגֹאֲלוֹ יְהֹוָה צְבָאוֹת אֲנִי רִאשׁוֹן וַאֲנִי אַחֲרוֹן וּמִבַּלְעָדַי אֵין אֱלֹהִים:

"So has G-d, King and Redeemer of Israel said, I am first and I am last and besides Me there is no other god."

In a metaphorical sense, what G-d is saying to us is that when things are going wrong, when we are in trouble, then He is *the first* One you turn to for help. However, when things are going well, then He is *the last* One you turn to. He is the last One on your mind, when it *seems* that you may not need help.

Our goal is awareness. We need to recognize that He is always there and we always need Him and His help – in good times, bad times and in the in-between times.

As a matter of fact, as we recite the litany of the confessional on *Yom Kippur*, known as *"Al Cheit,"* we say:

על חטא שחטאנו לפניך

We stand before G-d and declare that we did every sin *in His presence,* and for this we are eternally sorry and beg

His forgiveness. We stand before G-d. That is it: WE STAND BEFORE G-D. Every single place we stand, He is with us. He is there in our darkest hour, and He is there during our moments of joy. As long as we recognize that He is with us, our lives can mature, grow, prosper and be imbued with blessings.

Chapter 9

≈ Image One ≈

Although I lived in Chicago, many of the members of my shul and community were originally New Yorkers; and, as a result, they regularly quoted the *New York Times*. After first resisting, I finally subscribed to this paper so I would be able to connect to the various stories I heard.

Among all the sections I did read, the one that I never looked at was the obituaries. Since most people I knew who passed away did not have their obituaries printed, the chances that I would know someone listed in them was remote.

However, during one reading session, as I turned past the obituary section, my eye caught a particular death notice. To this day, I am not sure why I was drawn to it. In any case, there were actually two notices for the same person – one written by her daughter and one by her grandson.

The woman's name was Doris Weiss, and on September 2, 2003 the following obituaries appeared in the *New York Times*:

WEISS-Doris. *We were more than just mother and daughter; we were best friends, the two of us, a circle of love, never to be broken, never to be forgotten. Our mornings spent doing the Times crossword, 12 daily phone calls back and forth, driving around doing our errands together, winters on Fisher Island and, of course, spending your 70th in Paris. All this and* *so much more will deeply be missed. These past 18 months I have been so proud of you as I fought beside you for your life. I let you go now with my blessing so that your suffering may end. You have given me the greatest gift a daughter could receive in your never-ending love and I pass this on to my children and future grandchildren. I love you. You are in my heart forever. Love, Wendy*

And then the one from Doris' grandson:

WEISS-Doris. *Grandma, you have been as much a mother to me as my own. Our daily phone calls have instilled in me a strong sense of who I am today and who I want to become. Your spirit lives on in me and will be perpetuated in my children. I love you so much. Your first-born grandson, Joshua*

Listen to the beautiful messages declared in these lines. The daughter, Wendy, describes the daily contact with her mother and how she stood by her mother's side during her battle to live. She also speaks of her desire to pass these values on – the ones she learned from her mother – to her own children and grandchildren.

Then, the grandson, Joshua, describes something that immediately shows how he has already absorbed these values. He speaks of seeing his grandmother as his mother, their daily contact and his desire to pass these values and lessons on to his children.

All of these feelings and hopes that we strive for in this world were found in the obituaries:

Love
Acceptance
Value
Meaning
Tradition

The most remarkable part is that these words were shared with the entire world -for all others to see and learn from.

What can we learn, and why is this an "image" at all?

If the relationship with your family is not ideal – if it is not one of love, acceptance or value – do not wait until an obituary to express your feelings. By then, it will be too late. If you do not get along with your family, if you feel out of place, or if you ask yourself, "Am I really a part of this family?", then it is time to take to heart the words of these obituaries. It is time to imagine the relationship between the mother and daughter and the grandmother and grandson and to think about what it means in your life.

While this sounds like a nice lesson in family dynamics, what does it have to do with *Yom Kippur*? If you want your Father in Heaven to change His relationship with you, and if you want to change your relationship with Him, you need to work on your relationship with your own family. How we relate to our parents, siblings and close relatives affects how we relate to *Hashem* and He to us.

While this idea is appropriate for *Yom Kippur*, it is even more important in the days leading up to the holiest day of the year. When we make amends to our family members, essentially, we are getting our house in order, so that we may gain favor in the eyes of *Hashem*. It is then that our Father in Heaven will be more inclined to enable us to make amends with Him, as well.

For those who can identify with the obituary, you should count your blessings and keep on course. For those who cannot, some introspection is a good thing – especially when it can help mend family relationships and the relationship with G-d.

≈ Image Two ≈

The next image is that of a car – an ordinary car on an ordinary street in the city of Jerusalem, Israel.

I was in the *Givat Shaul* neighborhood of Jerusalem and needed to get to Emek Refaim Street in the German Colony neighborhood, a bus trip of about 40 minutes. I decided to go to the Central Bus Station and take a bus from there to my destination. Once I was aboard, I realized that part of its route went down Agrippas Street in the heart of *Shuk* (market) *Machane Yehuda*. Due to congestion, this short distance of only a few blocks would add an extra 35 minutes to my ride. As we approached the crowded street, I silently berated myself for having taken this bus in the first place. The bus arrived at King George and Agron streets, where I expected the driver to continue down to Keren Hayesod and on to Emek Refaim. Instead, he made a left turn and headed towards the Old City. I did not know that the bus route had been changed only a few days before my journey.

In a huff, I jumped up and along with others asked to be let off immediately, rather than at the next stop down the long hill. Surprisingly, the driver agreed, and a few of us got off the bus. By the time I made it to Emek Refaim, I was at least an hour late for my appointment.

It took me a little while to calm down, and, although delayed, I kept my meeting as planned. It was near the time to daven *Mincha*, and I headed to a nearby *shul* to check on the exact prayer time. As I walked towards the *shul*, I inadvertently turned my head and looked across the street. Just at that moment, I saw a car backing up right into a baby carriage being pushed by a mom, who was oblivious to the imminent danger. I shouted and the car stopped abruptly. I shudder to think what would have happened had I not been there.

Hashem put me in the right place at the right time. I understood at that moment why I needed to be on that bus. That is why I was delayed...

On *Yom Kippur*, it is that image that makes me stop and consider no matter what I try to do, and no matter what any of us attempt to do, we must remember

רבות מחשבות בלב איש ועצת הד' היא תקום

"Man has many thoughts and many intentions, but ultimately, it is the will of G-d that will prevail."

We often get upset when things do not "go our way." At times, we get angry when we can't find that parking spot or when we do not see the person we had planned to meet at a certain time. We are forced to change our original plans. However, the reality is that it is not "our plan" in the first place. We may have intentions to go somewhere, do something or acquire an object; but all of life is in the hands of *Hashem*. As we contemplate this on *Yom Kippur*, or any other day of the year, we can gain a sense of peace in our lives when things seem to go awry.

≈ Image Three ≈

The last image is a train.

Many years ago, I worked at a company that I was able to commute to by train. Day after day, I would drive to the station, park my car, walk up the stairs to the platform and await the train's arrival. I did this mechanically and without much thought every day.

One day, I noticed something interesting about the other commuters who seemed to have the same routine. They, too, would park their cars, climb the stairs and await the arrival of the train. I observed that some of them walked down to the far end of the platform on the left side, others walked to the far end on the right side, and yet others positioned themselves right in the middle.

I observed this day in and day out, but I could not figure out the thought process they used in choosing where to stand. I could understand if the platform areas were less crowded. I could also understand where they chose to stand, if there was some protection from the elements. But neither was the case.

Then it hit me. I observed the next step of their journey and it all made sense. As I watched through the window, I saw that some of the people got off the train car that was closest to the stairs they used to exit the station. This meant that where they positioned themselves to get on the train determined where they got off the train. It meant that there was a calculated thought process and a plan.

Where they got on determined where they would be let off. That thought and that image are actually quite powerful when we look at it through the lens of the Torah and *mitzvot*. We enter this world and are bidden to accomplish many things in life. Where we choose to stand, and with whom we choose to stand, will determine where we will "get off" from that journey into the Next World.

Chapter 10

≈ IMAGE ONE ≈

I want to share the following powerful, well-known quotes from Marc Levy (If Only It Were True, Atria Books, 2005) *"Imagine there is a bank that credits your account each morning with $86,400. It carries over no balance from day to day, allows you to keep no cash balance, and every evening cancels whatever part of the amount you had failed to use during the day. What would you do? Draw out every cent, of course! Well, everyone has such a bank. Its name is TIME.

Every morning, it credits you with 86,400 seconds. Every night it writes off, as lost, whatever of this you have failed to invest to good purpose. Each night it burns the records of the day. If you fail to use the day's deposits, the loss is yours. There is no going back. There is no drawing against the "tomorrow." You must live in the present on today's deposits. Invest it so as to get from it the utmost in health, happiness and success!! The clock is running. Make the most of today...

To realize the value of ONE YEAR: Ask a student who has failed his final exam.

To realize the value of ONE MONTH: Ask a mother who has given birth to a premature baby.

To realize the value of ONE WEEK: Ask an editor of a weekly newspaper.

To realize the value of ONE DAY: Ask a daily wage laborer who has ten kids to feed.

To realize the value of ONE HOUR: Ask the lovers who are waiting to meet.

To realize the value of ONE MINUTE: Ask the person who has missed the train.

To realize the value of ONE SECOND: Ask the person who has survived an accident.

To realize the value of ONE MILLISECOND: Ask the person who has won a silver medal in the Olympics.

Treasure every moment that you have!"

The first time that I read this piece, I just sat there. Then I read it again and again and again. The words, the image, the emotion it evokes, are all so powerful. I got to thinking about the "bank" of time we are given not only every day but the time we are given for our lives on this Earth. This "bank" works like a conventional bank, as well. We make deposits and add to our lives by doing *mitzvot* that are between man and G-d and between man and his fellow man. These deposits are put into our account on a minute-by-minute basis. When we perform an act against G-d's will, our account is debited.

We even earn interest on our deposits like in a regular bank. That interest is earned when other people emulate our positive qualities in service to *Hashem*. We are credited every time other people perform even the slightest *mitzvah* that we instructed them to do. Every time our actions influence others, interest is deposited into our account.

However, unlike a real bank, interest in the heavenly bank can be deducted from our account. If we influence another to go against G-d's will, then we carry a portion of that blame and responsibility with us. The result in this case is a reduction of our "earned interest" from the account.

When we contemplate the upcoming year, we do not need to think only in terms of 365 days. It is up to us and our actions to help determine our length of stay here on Earth. We have opportunities every minute of every day to make continuous deposits. As long as we are aware of that, we will be able to add to our account at all times, until *Hashem* decides it is time to make the final reckoning and close our account.

≈ Image Two ≈

The second image is a star.

Light travels at approximately 186,000 miles per second. A light year is the amount of distance light travels in one year. If you do the math, light travels approximately 5.89 trillion miles each year.

The closest star to Earth is Proxima Centauri. This star is 4.3 light years away from us. If there were to be a cosmic explosion on that star, we would not know about it for many years, as it would take the light many years to travel through space until we could observe it here on Earth. Similarly, if there were cosmic activity on the sun, such as sunspots, it would take about 8 minutes until we would be able to observe it here on Earth.

If there were to be a catastrophic event in space, such as a star exploding (which *does* actually happen fairly often), we would not know about it until hundreds of years later when the first light of that event were to reach us on Earth.

When we look into the sky and observe the stars, we are actually taking a peek back in time. The light emanating from these stars left their source a long time ago. I often wonder how many of the stars we see in the night sky are not even there anymore.

Chapter 10 | 95

How is the subject of stars dealt with in the Torah?

The very first mention of stars is in *Breishit* (Genesis) regarding the creation of the World, where it states:

וַיַּעַשׂ אֱלֹהִים אֶת־שְׁנֵי הַמְּאֹרֹת הַגְּדֹלִים אֶת־הַמָּאוֹר הַגָּדֹל לְמֶמְשֶׁלֶת הַיּוֹם וְאֶת־הַמָּאוֹר הַקָּטֹן לְמֶמְשֶׁלֶת הַלַּיְלָה וְ**אֵת הַכּוֹכָבִים** (בראשית א,טז)

"And God made the two large luminaries; the large one to rule the day and the smaller one to rule the night, and the stars" (Genesis 1:16)

Here we see that the Sun and the Moon are given a purpose as well as a job. The purpose is to light up the day and night skies. Later, we are told that they will help us reckon seasons, months, etc. Yet, when the Torah tells us about the creation of the stars, it does not mention their purpose, job or goal.

Later on, we begin to get a clue about the purpose of the stars when *Hashem* first reveals Himself to Avraham Avinu:

וַיּוֹצֵא אֹתוֹ הַחוּצָה וַיֹּאמֶר הַבֶּט־נָא הַשָּׁמַיְמָה וּסְפֹר הַכּוֹכָבִים אִם־תּוּכַל לִסְפֹּר אֹתָם וַיֹּאמֶר לוֹ כֹּה יִהְיֶה זַרְעֶךָ" (בראשית טו,ה)

He took [Avram] outside and said, "Look toward the heaven and count the stars. See if you can count them." [G-d then] said to him, "This is how your offspring will be." (Genesis 15:5)

The stars are to be used as a benchmark. We are to look at them and think of the promise that *Hashem* made to Avraham as to how numerous the Jewish people would become.

If we look at when *Hashem* reveals Himself for the first time to Yitzchak Avinu, once again, we see that *Hashem* invokes the stars:

וְהִרְבֵּיתִי אֶת־זַרְעֲךָ כְּכוֹכְבֵי הַשָּׁמַיִם וְנָתַתִּי לְזַרְעֲךָ אֵת כָּל־הָאֲרָצֹת הָאֵל וְהִתְבָּרֲכוּ בְזַרְעֲךָ כֹּל גּוֹיֵי הָאָרֶץ (בראשית כו,ד)

"I will make your offspring as numerous as the stars in the sky, and I will give your offspring all these lands. All the nations on earth shall bless themselves through your offspring." (Genesis 26:4)

And finally, when *Hashem* reveals Himself to Yaakov, He once again invokes stars and Bilaam himself says:

דָּרַךְ כּוֹכָב מִיַּעֲקֹב וְקָם שֵׁבֶט מִיִּשְׂרָאֵל (במדבר כד, יז)

("A star has gone forth from Jacob, and a staff will arise from Israel (Numbers 24:17).

Why all this talk of stars?

A hint may be found in the statement *Hashem* made at the first revelation to Avraham: "Look toward the heaven and count the stars"…

The Midrash tells us that Avraham went outside and actually began to count them. He attempted the impossible, and to *this Hashem* said: "This is how your offspring will be."

Avraham's children…*you and me.* We will look at what seems an impossible mission and will still attempt to accomplish it; but even if we cannot accomplish it, we will make the effort to begin.

The dual meaning of stars and the significance of the personal changes that we attempt to make on *Yom Kippur* are stark. As the "stars" of *Hashem* in this world, we will leave our mark on this world long after we are gone. There may be things that we do today in the service of *Hashem* that will not be felt or recognized for generations. Yet, it is our responsibility to take action and do what we need to do.

Another lesson that we can derive from Avraham and the stars is that we have a challenge before us at the beginning of every new year. We look back at a year that was and at all the things we have done and have not done, and we may feel overwhelmed. We may think that doing *teshuva* for everything is impossible. Yet, we realize that G-d blessed us that we should be like the stars and should emulate Avraham and all of our forefathers.

Avraham understood that the mission he was embarking upon of spreading the idea of monotheism was no small feat. As a matter of fact, it was a mission impossible; but the enormity of the mission did not stop him from trying. It did not stop him from attempting to do what was asked of him.

It says in Pirke Avot (Ethics of the Fathers) לא עליך המלאכה לגמור. This means that it is not incumbent upon you to finish a task, but you must still attempt to do your best to work on that task.

The same goes for us. We may think that doing *teshuva* is too hard. Yet, as Avraham did thousands of years ago, we stand up in *shul* and declare in unison: אשמנו, בגדנו, גזלנו (we have been guilty, we have betrayed, we have stolen…). We have made many mistakes, but we need to start somewhere; even if we do not fulfill our task completely.

This idea is also evident in *Parashat Korach*. After Moshe and Aharon are challenged by Korach and his followers, it is made clear to all *Bnei Yisrael* that the true leaders – the ones whom *Hashem* had already chosen – are Moshe and Aharon. In order to prove this to the people, every leader of Israel is told to place his staff in front of the *Ohel Moed* (the Tent of Meeting). The staff of the one whom G-d has chosen as the true leader will miraculously bud and bloom. And, indeed, it was Aharon's staff that budded and bloomed.

וַיְהִי מִמָּחֳרָת וַיָּבֹא מֹשֶׁה אֶל־אֹהֶל הָעֵדוּת וְהִנֵּה פָּרַח מַטֵּה־אַהֲרֹן לְבֵית לֵוִי וַיֹּצֵא פֶרַח וַיָּצֵץ צִיץ וַיִּגְמֹל שְׁקֵדִים: (במדבר יז,כג)

And it came to pass on the morrow, that Moshe went into the tent of the testimony; and, behold, the staff of Aharon for the house of Levi was budded, and put forth buds, and bloomed blossoms, and bore ripe almonds. (Numbers 17:23)

If the staff of Aharon produced almonds, why was it necessary to tell us that it also blossomed? Because that is the lesson we need to hear. Our job – represented by the flowering blossoms – is to make the *hishtadlut* (effort) to achieve what we can. We need to take the steps. We do not have to complete the job. We need to take those significant steps towards *teshuva* and act on them. Will we accomplish a complete repentance? Perhaps, but even if we are unable to do so, we must take steps and make that effort. That is part of the message of *Yom Kippur*.

It is never too late…

≈ Image Three ≈

The final image is a shadow.

I often went to daven at the *Kotel HaMaaravi* (the Western Wall) during our pre-Aliya summer trips to Israel. It was there that I, along with thousands of my fellow Jews, would find solace in reciting the *Tefillot* and feel a real connection to G-d.

On one particularly hot afternoon, I went to daven *Mincha* at the *Kotel* and decided to stand in a shaded corner. As I prepared to daven, I suddenly realized that I was standing face-to-face with a metaphor for our relationship with *Hashem*.

When we stand alone and are out in the "heat of the sun" with our problems and troubles, we often feel lonely – as if we are almost melting. The longer we stand alone in "the sun," the hotter we feel, the worse we feel and the thirstier we get.

What are we thirsting for? What is the cause of this pain and suffering? We are thirsting for solace and comfort – for help to protect us from the scorching heat. It is this heat and loneliness that contribute to the pain and the suffering.

Just as I had walked into the cool shade of the *Kotel* to find relief from the sun, we have that same opportunity in our daily life. Instead of feeling the pain of loneliness, suffering and despair or wallowing in our past sins, there is shade into which we can move to find comfort, contentment, hope and joy. That is the shade provided by *Hashem's* presence in our lives.

King David tells us in *Tehillim* 91:1:

יֹשֵׁב בְּסֵתֶר עֶלְיוֹן בְּצֵל שַׁדַּי יִתְלוֹנָן: (תהלים צא,א)

"He who dwells in the shelter of the Most High will rest in the shade of the Almighty"

The metaphor of the shade is indicative of the peaceful and protective shelter that G-d provides for us, if we are willing to bask in that shelter. Sometimes a person chooses to remain miserable. Sometimes a person may think there is no other course in life and that he is stuck in "the scorching sun." G-d comes along to tell us that He is there for us. He beckons us to join Him in His shade and allow Him to assuage that which is troubling us.

On the holiest day of the year, *Yom Kippur*, we open our eyes and reflect on the year that was. Maybe all we can see is the pain, the sin and the sadness of the prior year. Maybe, in our mind's eye, we foresee yet another year of this. We might even ask ourselves, as King David did in *Tehillim* 121, from where will my protection come?

As so often happens in life, the answer is right in front of us and all around us. G-d is there to provide that shelter. G-d is there to give us solace.

G-d is there to say, as he did in *Bamidbar* 21: סלחתי כדבריך – I have forgiven you as you have requested.

GLOSSARY

HEBREW	ENGLISH
Achdut	Unity
Ahavat Hashem	Love of G-d
Ahavat Yisrael	Love of one's fellow Jew
Al Cheit	Litany of sins recited on Yom Kippur (Lit. "on the sin…")
Aliya	Immigrating to Israel
Aseret Y'Mai Teshuva	See *Yamim Noraim*
Aliya L'regel	Act of coming to Jerusalem on the major holidays in time of Temple
Aufruf	A bridegroom called to the Torah on the Shabbat prior to his wedding (Yiddish)
Av	The fifth Hebrew month
Avinu Malkenu	A special penitential prayer recited on certain days (Lit. "Our Father Our King")
Avraham	The patriarch Abraham
Baal Teshuva	One who returns to a traditional Torah-based life
Bein Adam L'Chavero	Between man and his fellow man
Bein Adam L'Makom	Between man and G-d
Beit Knesset	Shul/Synagogue
Bet HaMikdash	The Temple that stood in Jerusalem
Bnei Yisrael	The Jewish People
Breishit	The first of the Five Books of the Torah
Brit Milah	Ritual circumcision
Chazzan	Cantor
Chuppa	Wedding canopy
Daf Yomi	Program of learning the entire Talmud one page a day for 7 1/2 years
Daven	Pray
David HaMelech	King David

Derashot	Biblical exegesis
Divrei Torah	Explanations and talks based on the words of Torah
Eishet Chayil	Woman of Valor--refers to one's wife (based on sentence in Proverbs)
Elul	Sixth Hebrew month
Emuna	Faith
Erev Shabbat	Friday, the eve of the Sabbath
Erev Yom Kippur	Yom Kippur Eve
Ezer K'negdo	Lit. "His helpmate opposite him" (a man's wife)
Gemara	See *Talmud*
HaKadosh Baruch Hu	"The Holy One, blessed be His Name" (G-d)
Hashem	"The Name" (refers to G-d)
Hashgacha Pratit	Personal oversight by G-d
Hishtadlut	Making a concerted effort
Katyushas	Rockets
Kedoshim	The "holy ones" (those murdered for being Jewish)
Kehilla	Community
Ketubot	Name of one of the Tractates of the Talmud
Kippah	Yarmulke/skullcap
Kivnei Maron	Lit. "Like sheep line up" (refers to how G-d "reviews" all humans on Rosh Hashana
Kol Nidre	The name of the prayer service on the night of Yom Kippur
Kollel	Advanced study group (generally with married men) learning Talmud
Korach	A man who challenged the authority of Moses and Aharon
Kotel	Western Wall in Jerusalem
Kotzker Rebbe	Sainted rabbi from the town of Kotzk

GLOSSARY

Lashon Hara	Speaking ill of another person
Maariv/Arvit	Evening prayers
Machatzit HaShekel	A half-shekel coin used in the time of the Temple
Machzor	Prayer book used for High Holidays
Mesorah	Tradition
Mikveh	Ritual bath used for purifying oneself
Mincha	Afternoon prayers
Mishkan	Tabernacle
Mitzva/Mitzvot	Commandment(s) from Hashem
Mussaf	Additional prayers in shul on Shabbat and holidays
Parashat Korach	One of the weekly Torah readings entitled "Korach"
Pasuk	A verse in the Torah
Purim	Holiday celebrating the Jews being saved from Haman
Rosh Chodesh	First day(s) of the new Hebrew Month
Rosh Hashana	Jewish New Year
Sefer Melachim	Book of Kings
Sefer Orchot Tzadikim	Book entitled "Ways of the Righteous"
Sefer Yeshayahu	Book of Isaiah
Seudat Chag	Special meal eaten on holidays
Shabbat	Sabbath
Shacharit	Morning prayers
Shalom Zachor	Celebration on the first Friday night after a male child is born
Shel Yad	Tefillin that is worn on the arm
Shema	Prayer/article of faith that expresses belief in Oneness of G-d
Shemona Esrei	Central prayer of all prayer services
Shtender	Lectern (Yiddish)
Shul	Shul (Yiddish)
Simcha	A happy occasion
Sivan	Third Hebrew month

Sukkot	Feast of Tabernacles
Talmud	Central text of Rabbinic Judaism
Tammuz	Fourth Hebrew month
Tefilla/Tefillot	Prayer/prayers
Tefillat HaDerech	Traveler's prayer
Tefillin	Phylacteries (worn on arm and head)
Tehillim	Psalms
Teshuva	Repentance
Tishrei/Tishri	Seventh Hebrew month (includes Rosh Hashana and Yom Kippur)
U'netaneh Tokef	Special prayer recited in the Mussaf service on Rosh Hashana and Yom Kippur
Yamim Noraim	Days of Awe (From Rosh Hashana through Yom Kippur)
Yishtabach	A prayer in the morning services
Yom HaKadosh	The Holy Day (Another name for Yom Kippur)
Yom Kippur	Day of Atonement (holiest day on the Jewish calendar)
Zaydeh	Grandfather